STARTERS ACTIVITIES

Presents

Macdonald Educational

About Starters Activities

These books cover a variety of activities for children at school or at home. The projects with their step-by-step illustrations, require the minimum of help from teachers or parents. Most of the words in the text will be in the reading vocabulary of the majority of young readers. Word and sentence length have also been carefully controlled. Extra information and more complex activities are included at the end of each book. Where possible, the child is free to invent and experiment on his own, but concise instructions are given wherever necessary. Teachers and experts have been consulted on the content and accuracy of these books.

Illustrated by: Ann Knight

Managing Editor: Su Swallow

Editor: Diana Finley

Production: Stephen Pawley, Vivienne Driscoll

Reading consultant: Donald Moyle, author of The Teaching of Reading and senior lecturer in education at Edge Hill College of Education

Chairman, teacher advisory panel: F. F. Blackwell, director of the primary extension programme, National Council for Educational Technology

Teacher panel: Stephanie Connell, Sally Chaplin, Margaret Anderson

Colour reproduction by:
Colourcraftsmen Limited

Filmsetting by:
Layton-Sun Limited

© Macdonald and Company
(Publishers) Limited 1974
ISBN 0 356 04926 4
Made and printed in Great Britain by:
Adams Bros. and Shardlow Ltd, Leicester

First published in 1974 by
Macdonald Educational
St Giles House
49-50 Poland Street
London W1

Contents

This book is about making presents.
People always like presents
you have made yourself.

stones

wool

paper

buttons

Paperweight

Find stones that have funny shapes.
Paint patterns or faces on them
with thick paint.

2

Use the paperweight on a table.
It will stop the papers blowing away.

food tray

card

sticky tape

Flower Basket

Find a silver foil food tray.
Make a handle out of card.
Fix the handle to the tray.

4

paper

twigs

Lay twigs at the bottom of the basket.
Wrap strips of paper round your finger.
Twist one end to make the stalk.
Stick the flowers between the twigs.

5

Basket

Here is another basket you can make.
You will need a square piece of wood
and straight twigs the same length.

6

wood glue

Glue the sticks onto the square like this.
Put a pot inside your basket.
This would make a good Easter present.

glue

felt

buttons

Purse

Make this purse out of felt.
Stick the two sides.
Decorate it with buttons and beads.

8

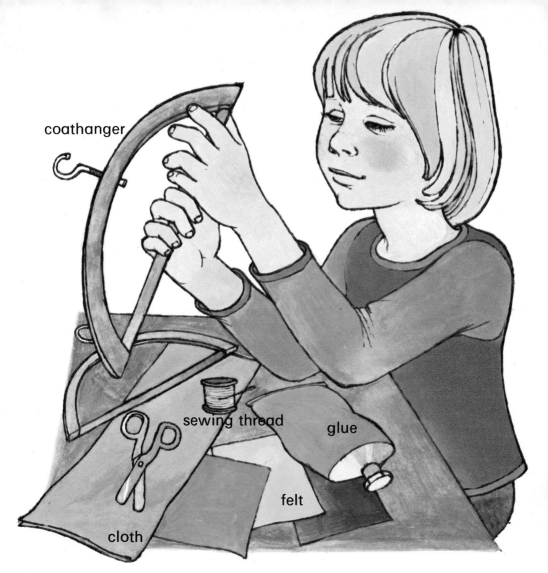

coathanger

sewing thread

glue

felt

cloth

Knitting Bag
You will need these things
to make a knitting bag.
It can be stuck or sewn together.

Cut a long piece of cloth
the same width as the coathangers.
Take out the hooks.
Then fix a coathanger to each end.

Now fold the cloth
and sew or stick the sides.
Stick on a felt flower like this.

11

Draught-stopper

Cut a leg from some old tights
to make a snake.
Fill it with other old tights.

12

When the snake is full, tie up the end.
Sew on eyes and a long tongue.
Try making other animals
in the same way.

13

holes

card

hole puncher

string

Recipe Book

This book is for keeping recipes.
Use white card for the cover.
Then you can decorate it.

14

Polyfilla paste

thick paint

card comb

Cut a comb out of card like this.
Paste one side of the cover.
Dip the comb into thick paint.
Make patterns in the paste.

15

silver foil

Paper Jewellery
You can make jewellery out of paper
and silver foil.
Use coloured paper.
16

sticky tape

Fix the brooch with a safety pin.
Use paper clips for the bracelet
and headband.

17

Sweet Boat
This boat is made out of
a cardboard box.
Use a tube for the funnel.
18

Now fill the boat up with sweets.
Share this present with your friends.

19

Money Box

Make a Noah's Ark money box.
Use a date box for the ark
and a matchbox for the cabin.

20

card

pipecleaners

Make a hole for your money.
Make some pairs of animals.

Presents words

paper-weight
(page 2)

patterns
(page 2)

basket
(page 4)

handle
(page 4)

twigs
(page 5)

strips
(page 5)

stalk
(page 5)

wood
(page 6)

purse
(page 8)

comb
(page 15)

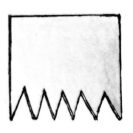

decorate
(page 8)

jewellery
(page 16)

coathanger
(page 9)

funnel
(page 18)

**draught-
stopper**
(page 12)

cabin
(page 20)

23

Remember

Use the right glue
for what you are sticking.
A paper paste
will not work well
for wood.

Never leave sharp things
lying around.
Put scissors and knives
somewhere safe.
Stick needles and pins
into a pin-cushion.

Put newspaper on tables
if you are using glue
or paints.

Clear away afterwards
Put scraps of paper
and rubbish in the dustbin.

24

Some harder projects

Wool belt

Find some pieces of different coloured thick wools, about 1 metre long. Divide them into three groups of five strands of wool. Tie a knot at the end of each group. Comb the strands together with your fingers. Then tie the three groups of wool together, close to the first knots. Plait the three groups together neatly. Tie a knot when you reach about 5 centimetres from the far end of the belt. Cut two round shapes from felt. Cut out letters from a different colour felt. If you are giving the belt to someone, you could use their initials. Stick one initial onto each of the felt circles. Fix the circles onto each end of the belt.

Rag dolls

Cut lots of circles of material about 8 centimetres across. You will need lots of them so use old remnants and scraps. Sew big tacking stitches all around the circle about $\frac{1}{2}$ centimetre from the edge. Then pull gently on the thread until the circle is pulled into a frill. Fasten the thread firmly. Do this with all the other circles. Thread the frills together to form the body, arms and legs of the doll. Paint a face on a ping pong ball for the doll's head. Stick the head on the body with a strong glue.

Some harder projects

Paper beads

You can use almost any paper to make beads. Bright wrapping paper or wallpaper is good. You can also use white paper and paint the beads. Cut the paper into strips about $1\frac{1}{2}$ centimetres wide and 20 centimetres long. Cut the ends into a slightly pointed shape. Paste the strips with paper paste or with a flour and water mixture. Roll the strips up tightly. Leave the beads to dry. Thread the beads onto strong cotton. You can make necklaces, bracelets and headbands this way.

Animal 'Snap' Cards

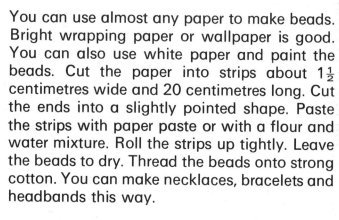

Find some wrapping paper with pictures of animals. You could look for animal pictures in magazines and comics too. You must have two of every animal you find. Cut out the animals and stick them on pieces of card about 6 centimetres wide and 8 centimetres long. You will need at least ten pairs of cards. Play this game with a friend in the same way as ordinary 'Snap'.

Paperclip jewellery

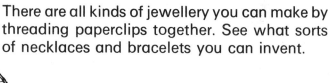

There are all kinds of jewellery you can make by threading paperclips together. See what sorts of necklaces and bracelets you can invent.